RISOTTO

RISOTTO

CLIVE TRING

p

This is a Parragon Publishing Book

First published in 2005

Parragon Publishing
Queen Street House
4 Queen Street
Bath BA1 1HE, UK

ISBN: 1-40544-757-5

Printed in China

Produced by the Bridgewater Book Company Ltd
Photographer: Laurie Evans
Home Economist: Annie Rigg

Notes for the Reader
This book uses imperial, metric, or US cup measurements. Follow the same units of measurement throughout; do not mix imperial and metric. All spoon measurements are level: teaspoons are assumed to be 5 ml, and tablespoons are assumed to be 15 ml. Unless otherwise stated, milk is assumed to be whole, eggs and individual vegetables such as potatoes are medium, and pepper is freshly ground black pepper. Recipes using raw or very lightly cooked eggs should be avoided by infants, the elderly, pregnant women, convalescents, and anyone suffering from an illness. The times given are an approximate guide only. Preparation times differ according to the techniques used by different people and the cooking times may also vary from those given. Optional ingredients, variations, or serving suggestions have not been included in the calculations.

Picture acknowledgments
The Bridgewater Book Company would like to thank the following for permission to reproduce copyright material: Getty Images, pages 6, 8, 24, and endpapers; Corbis Images, pages 44, 64, 83.

CONTENTS

Risotto, meaning "little rice," is unique among rice dishes. Firstly, unlike, say, pilaf, all the ingredients are usually cooked with the rice rather than the two parts of the dish being combined at the end. Secondly, risotto has a special creamy texture; the rice is moist yet still has a "bite." This is mainly because it is based on specific varieties of rice that are grown in northern Italy. In fact, Italian rice was once protected from export by law. However, this didn't prevent United States' founding father Thomas Jefferson from smuggling out sacks of it to plant on his estate in Virginia.

The rice used for risotto is a white, starchy, medium grain that can absorb far more liquid than long-grain rice. Of the four types of rice grown in Italy, only superfino or fino are suitable. The best-known and most widely available superfino is Arborio, which has a slightly nutty flavor. Other suitable varieties include Carnaroli, Baldo, Roma, Maratelli, and the fino Vialone Nano.

INTRODUCTION

The technique for preparing risotto is as much the key to successful results as using the right rice. Onion, garlic, and, perhaps, other vegetables are briefly cooked in butter or butter and oil, then the rice is added to the pan. Risotto rice is never rinsed first, as this would wash away a lot of the essential starch. Once in the pan, it is stirred until all the grains are thoroughly coated and glistening before any liquid, such as wine and stock, is added. A good-quality stock is crucial and it should be simmering gently before it is added—very gradually—to the rice. Add a ladleful of hot stock and cook, stirring constantly, until it has been completely absorbed, then add another

ladleful and keep stirring, and so on. The rice should never become dry and should be stirred throughout its cooking time, about 20–25 minutes. Although a quantity of liquid is specified in every recipe in this book, it is impossible to say exactly how much is required because it will vary depending on the type of rice. Making risotto properly does require practice, but you will soon learn to "feel" when it is exactly al dente.

The final touch is to beat in the *mantecatura*—a tablespoon of butter and, often, some freshly grated Parmesan or other cheese. This gives the risotto its typical extra creamy consistency. All traditional risotto recipes include butter both for the initial cooking and for stirring in at the end.

A large, heavy-bottom pan is important. The rice will treble in volume during cooking, so you need plenty of room to stir. As the heat is distributed evenly by a heavy-bottom pan, the rice is far less likely to stick or, worse still, burn.

You cannot make a satisfactory risotto in a skillet because the large surface area will cause too much evaporation.

As the following recipes demonstrate, risotti can include a vast range of different ingredients, from cheese to seafood and from vegetables to chicken. So once you have mastered the basic technique, the only limit is your imagination.

Some of the best Italian recipes—and that certainly includes risotti—are the simplest, using top-quality, seasonal ingredients in complementary combinations. The unique flavors of herbs, vegetables, mushrooms, and cheese are allowed to "sing out," balanced against the rich, creamy texture of the rice. As a result, these simple dishes are, in fact, rather fine and utterly delicious.

However, don't imagine that, just because they involve only a few, easily available ingredients, you can abandon the nicer points of risotto making. Indeed, their very simplicity demands the highest standard of cooking and you will find that your efforts are fully rewarded.

Almost all the recipes in this chapter are suitable for vegetarians, so although chicken stock is most commonly used for cooking risotti, the option of using vegetable stock is listed in the ingredients. Use either homemade or a

PART ONE
SIMPLY DELICIOUS

full-flavored ready-made version. French and Italian varieties tend to be particularly good.

Although these recipes are designed to be served as a main course, they would also work extremely well as the first course for a dinner party, providing a delightful contrast in flavor and texture to a meat- or fish-based dish to follow. If you are planning to do this, you can safely assume that a risotto for four will stretch to serving six as a first course—it is, after all, very filling. This is not at all authentic, as in Italy the first and second courses are of equal size and importance. Nevertheless, it is a delicious idea and, in any case, Italians wouldn't serve such large portions in the first place.

BASIC BASIL RISOTTO

SERVES 4

5 cups vegetable or
chicken stock

1 tbsp olive oil

3 tbsp butter

1 small onion,
finely chopped

10 fresh basil leaves,
chopped or shredded,
plus extra whole leaves
to garnish

4 tomatoes, seeded
and diced

4 oz/115 g green beans,
cut into 1-inch/2.5-cm
lengths and cooked

generous 1 3/8 cups
risotto rice

2 tbsp pine nuts

3/4 cup freshly grated
Parmesan or Grana
Padano cheese

salt and pepper

Bring the stock to a boil in a pan, then reduce the heat and keep simmering gently over low heat while you are cooking the risotto.

Heat the oil with 2 tablespoons of the butter in a deep pan over medium heat until the butter has melted. Stir in the onion, three-quarters of the basil, the tomatoes, and beans and cook gently for 2–3 minutes for the flavors to blend.

Reduce the heat, add the rice, and mix to coat in oil and butter. Cook, stirring constantly, for 2–3 minutes, or until the grains are translucent.

Gradually add the hot stock, a ladleful at a time. Stir constantly and add more liquid as the rice absorbs each addition. Increase the heat to medium so that the liquid bubbles. Cook for 20 minutes, or until all the liquid is absorbed and the rice is creamy. Season to taste.

While the risotto is cooking, heat a skillet over high heat. Add the pine nuts and dry-fry for 1–2 minutes, or until just starting to brown. Be careful not to let them burn.

Remove the risotto from the heat and add the remaining butter. Carefully fold in the remaining chopped basil. Mix well, then stir in the Parmesan until it melts.

Divide the risotto between 4 warmed plates and garnish with whole basil leaves and the pine nuts before serving.

BASIL LEAVES HAVE A DELICATE TEXTURE AND CAN BE BRUISED BY CHOPPING. AN ALTERNATIVE IS TO SHRED THEM INTO SMALL PIECES WITH YOUR FINGERS.

LEMON AND ROSEMARY RISOTTO

SERVES 4

2 lemons

5 cups vegetable or chicken stock

1 tbsp olive oil

3 tbsp butter

1 small onion, finely chopped

1 tbsp finely chopped fresh rosemary

generous 1³/₈ cups risotto rice

³/₄ cup freshly grated Parmesan or Grana Padano cheese

salt and pepper

Grate the lemon rinds and set aside. Squeeze the juice from the lemons into a small pan and place over medium heat until just about to boil.

Bring the stock to a boil in a pan, then reduce the heat and keep simmering gently over low heat while you are cooking the risotto.

Heat the oil with 2 tablespoons of the butter in a deep pan over medium heat until the butter has melted. Stir in the onion and half the rosemary and cook gently, stirring occasionally, for 5 minutes, or until the onion is soft and translucent. Do not brown.

Reduce the heat, add the rice, and mix to coat in oil and butter. Cook, stirring constantly, for 2–3 minutes, or until the grains are translucent.

Gradually add the hot stock, a ladleful at a time, alternating with the lemon juice. Stir constantly and add more liquid as the rice absorbs each addition. Increase the heat to medium so that the liquid bubbles. Cook for 20 minutes, or until all the liquid is absorbed and the rice is creamy. Season to taste with salt and pepper.

Remove the risotto from the heat and add the remaining butter and rosemary. Mix well, then stir in the Parmesan until it melts. Spoon the risotto onto individual plates and sprinkle with the grated lemon rind. Season and serve.

THE AVERAGE LEMON YIELDS ABOUT 4 TABLESPOONS OF JUICE, BUT THIS MAY VARY. THEREFORE, YOU MAY NOT NEED ALL THE STOCK IN THIS RECIPE. IN ANY CASE, DIFFERENT KINDS OF RISOTTO RICE WILL ABSORB DIFFERENT AMOUNTS OF LIQUID, SO, WHATEVER THE RECIPE, OBSERVE THE TEXTURE AS THE RICE COOKS. WHEN IT BECOMES CREAMY IT WILL BE READY, AND YOU SHOULD NOT ADD ANY MORE LIQUID.

PARMESAN CHEESE RISOTTO WITH MUSHROOMS

SERVES 4

4 cups vegetable or chicken stock

2 tbsp olive oil or vegetable oil

generous 1 cup risotto rice

2 garlic cloves, crushed

1 onion, chopped

2 celery stalks, chopped

1 red or green bell pepper, seeded and chopped

8 oz/225 g mushrooms, thinly sliced

1 tbsp chopped fresh oregano or 1 tsp dried oregano

1/4 cup sun-dried tomatoes in olive oil, drained and chopped (optional)

1/2 cup finely grated Parmesan cheese

salt and pepper

To garnish

fresh flat-leaf parsley sprigs or bay leaves

Bring the stock to a boil in a pan, then reduce the heat and keep simmering gently over low heat while you are cooking the risotto.

Heat the oil in a deep pan. Add the rice and cook over low heat, stirring constantly, for 2–3 minutes, until the grains are thoroughly coated in oil and translucent.

Add the garlic, onion, celery, and bell pepper and cook, stirring frequently, for 5 minutes. Add the mushrooms and cook for 3–4 minutes. Stir in the oregano.

Gradually add the hot stock, a ladleful at a time. Stir constantly and add more liquid as the rice absorbs each addition. Increase the heat to medium so that the liquid bubbles. Cook for 20 minutes, or until all the liquid is absorbed and the rice is creamy. Add the sun-dried tomatoes, if using, 5 minutes before the end of the cooking time and season to taste with salt and pepper.

Remove the risotto from the heat and stir in half the Parmesan until it melts. Transfer the risotto to warmed plates. Top with the remaining cheese, garnish with flat-leaf parsley or bay leaves, and serve at once.

FOR THE BEST FLAVOR, BUY PARMESAN CHEESE IN A SINGLE PIECE AND GRATE OR SHAVE IT AS REQUIRED. IT WILL KEEP FOR A LONG TIME IF IT IS WRAPPED IN FOIL AND STORED IN THE REFRIGERATOR. READY-GRATED PARMESAN CHEESE, ON THE OTHER HAND, QUICKLY LOSES ITS FLAVOR.

BLUE CHEESE RISOTTO

SERVES 4

5 cups vegetable or chicken stock

1 tbsp olive oil

3 tbsp butter

1 small onion, finely chopped

2 oz/55 g rindless bacon or vegetarian bacon slices, diced

generous 1³/8 cups risotto rice

4 oz/115 g Gorgonzola or dolcelatte cheese

salt and pepper

Bring the stock to a boil in a pan, then reduce the heat and keep simmering gently over low heat while you are cooking the risotto.

Heat the oil with 2 tablespoons of the butter in a deep pan over low heat until the butter has melted. Stir in the onion and bacon and cook, stirring occasionally, for 5 minutes, or until the bacon is just starting to brown and the onion is soft.

Add the rice and mix to coat in oil and butter. Cook, stirring constantly, for 2–3 minutes, or until the grains are translucent.

Gradually add the hot stock, a ladleful at a time. Stir constantly and add more liquid as the rice absorbs each addition. Increase the heat to medium so that the liquid bubbles. Cook for 20 minutes, or until all the liquid is absorbed and the rice is creamy. Season to taste.

Remove the risotto from the heat and add the remaining butter. Mix well, then crumble in half the blue cheese and stir well until it melts. Season well with plenty of pepper.

Spoon the risotto onto 4 warmed individual plates. Crumble or dice the remaining blue cheese and sprinkle it over the top of the risotto before serving.

ONE OF THE WORLD'S OLDEST VEINED CHEESES, GORGONZOLA IS A RICH CREAMY COLOR WITH DELICATE GREEN VEINING, ALTHOUGH IT IS ALWAYS KNOWN AS A BLUE CHEESE. IT HAS A PIQUANT BUT SUBTLY RICH FLAVOR AND AN APPETIZING AROMA. IF IT SMELLS BITTER, OR THE TEXTURE FEELS HARD AND DRY, DO NOT BUY IT. DOLCELATTE IS A CREAMIER, MILDER VERSION OF GORGONZOLA CREATED DURING THE 1960S.

CRUNCHY WALNUT RISOTTO

SERVES 4

5 cups vegetable or chicken stock

1 tbsp olive oil

2¹/₂ oz/70 g butter

1 small onion, finely chopped

generous 1³/₈ cups risotto rice

1 cup walnut halves

³/₄ cup freshly grated Parmesan or Grana Padano cheese

¹/₄ cup mascarpone cheese

2 oz/55 g Gorgonzola cheese, diced

salt and pepper

Bring the stock to a boil in a pan, then reduce the heat and keep simmering gently over low heat while you are cooking the risotto.

Heat the oil with 2 tablespoons of the butter in a deep pan over medium heat until the butter has melted. Add the onion and cook, stirring occasionally, for 5–7 minutes, or until soft and starting to turn golden. Do not brown.

Reduce the heat, add the rice, and mix to coat in oil and butter. Cook, stirring constantly, for 2–3 minutes, or until the grains are translucent.

Gradually add the hot stock, a ladleful at a time. Stir constantly and add more liquid as the rice absorbs each addition. Increase the heat to medium so that the liquid bubbles. Cook for 20 minutes, or until all the liquid is absorbed and the rice is creamy. Season to taste.

While the risotto is cooking, melt 2 tablespoons of the remaining butter in a skillet over medium heat. Add the walnuts and toss for 2–3 minutes, or until just starting to brown.

Remove the risotto from the heat and add the remaining butter. Mix well, then stir in the Parmesan, mascarpone, and Gorgonzola until they melt, along with most of the walnuts. Spoon the risotto onto warmed plates, sprinkle with the remaining walnuts, and serve.

RISOTTI, LIKE SOUFFLÉS, SHOULD NOT BE KEPT WAITING WHILE YOUR GUESTS COME TO THE TABLE. ONCE THE "MANTECATURA"—THE FINAL ADDITION, USUALLY BUTTER AND GRATED PARMESAN—HAS BEEN BEATEN IN TO MAKE THE TEXTURE EVEN CREAMIER, THE RISOTTO SHOULD BE SERVED.

SUNSHINE RISOTTO

SERVES 6

about 12 sun-dried
tomatoes

generous 6¹/₃ cups
chicken or vegetable stock

2 tbsp olive oil

1 large onion,
finely chopped

4–6 garlic cloves,
finely chopped

generous 1³/₄ cups
risotto rice

2 tbsp chopped fresh
flat-leaf parsley

1 cup freshly grated aged
romano cheese

extra virgin olive oil,
for drizzling

Place the sun-dried tomatoes in a heatproof bowl and pour over enough boiling water to cover. Set aside to soak for 30 minutes, or until soft and supple. Drain and pat dry with paper towels, then shred thinly and set aside.

Bring the stock to a boil in a pan, then reduce the heat and keep simmering gently over low heat while you are cooking the risotto.

Heat the olive oil in a deep pan over medium heat. Add the onion and cook, stirring occasionally, for 2 minutes, or until starting to soften. Add the garlic and cook for an additional 15 seconds.

Reduce the heat, add the rice, and mix to coat in oil. Cook, stirring constantly, for 2–3 minutes, or until the grains are translucent.

Gradually add the hot stock, a ladleful at a time. Stir constantly and add more liquid as the rice absorbs each addition. Increase the heat to

medium so that the liquid bubbles. After about 15 minutes, stir in the sun-dried tomatoes.

Continue adding the stock, stirring constantly, until the risotto has been cooking for 20 minutes, or until all the liquid is absorbed and the rice is creamy.

Remove the pan from the heat and stir in the chopped parsley and half the romano cheese. Spoon the risotto onto 6 warmed plates. Drizzle with extra virgin olive oil and sprinkle the remaining romano cheese on top. Serve at once.

ROMANO IS AN ITALIAN CHEESE MADE FROM SHEEP MILK. ALTHOUGH IT IS MADE ALL OVER ITALY, THE AGED ROMANO FROM SARDINIA IS PARTICULARLY FINE.

PUMPKIN AND CHESTNUT RISOTTO

SERVES 4

4 cups vegetable or chicken stock

I tbsp olive oil

3 tbsp butter

I small onion, finely chopped

8 oz/225 g pumpkin, diced

8 oz/225 g chestnuts, cooked and shelled

generous 1³/₈ cups risotto rice

²/₃ cup dry white wine

I tsp crumbled saffron threads (optional)

³/₄ cup freshly grated Parmesan or Grana Padano cheese

salt and pepper

Bring the stock to a boil, then reduce the heat and keep simmering gently over low heat while you are cooking the risotto.

Heat the oil with 2 tablespoons of the butter in a deep pan over medium heat until the butter has melted. Stir in the onion and pumpkin and cook, stirring occasionally, for 5 minutes, or until the onion is soft and starting to turn golden and the pumpkin begins to color.

Coarsely chop the chestnuts and add to the mixture. Stir thoroughly to coat.

Reduce the heat, add the rice, and mix to coat in oil and butter. Cook, stirring constantly, for 2–3 minutes, or until the grains are translucent. Add the wine and cook, stirring constantly, for I minute until it has reduced.

If using the saffron threads, dissolve them in 4 tablespoons of the hot stock and add the liquid to the rice after the wine has been absorbed. Cook, stirring constantly, until the liquid has been absorbed.

Gradually add the hot stock, a ladleful at a time. Stir constantly and add more liquid as the rice absorbs each addition. Increase the heat to medium so that the liquid bubbles. Cook for 20 minutes, or until all the liquid is absorbed and the rice is creamy. Season to taste.

Remove the risotto from the heat and add the remaining butter. Mix well, then stir in the Parmesan until it melts. Adjust the seasoning if necessary, spoon the risotto onto 4 warmed plates, and serve at once.

SAFFRON IS THE MOST EXPENSIVE SPICE IN THE WORLD, BUT IT HAS AN EXQUISITE AROMA AND FLAVOR AND, FORTUNATELY, YOU NEED TO USE VERY LITTLE. THERE IS NO ADEQUATE SUBSTITUTE.

Even those who are usually reluctant to eat their vegetables will be seduced by these wonderful vegetable, herb, and mushroom risotti, while those who are enthusiasts for a healthy diet will be spoilt for choice. It's the easiest way in the world to follow guidelines to include "five a day" in your family meals.

Freshness, as with all Italian cooking, is the keynote. Seasonal vegetables in peak condition are full of flavor and their vibrant colors are a feast for the eyes. The earthy, robust taste of wild mushrooms is always at its best in the fall, while fresh asparagus is a treat to savor in the spring and early summer.

This chapter also includes recipes for two risotti for "cheats": one that is baked in the oven, and one made with brown rice rather than risotto rice. For those occasions when you simply cannot spare the time to stay in the kitchen for the essential stirring of a traditional

PART TWO
THE GROCER'S FARE

risotto, these both make tasty and satisfactory substitutes. However, it's probably best not to serve them to an Italian friend!

Like the recipes in the first chapter, almost all of those here are perfect for vegetarians. As before, you can substitute a well-flavored vegetable stock for chicken stock.

Ideal for ringing the changes in the weekly family supper menu, these vegetable risotti are also great for informal and inexpensive entertaining. Seat your guests around the kitchen table, with a glass of wine each, so that they can admire your culinary skills as you effortlessly produce a small Italian masterpiece without missing any of the conversation.

RISOTTO PRIMAVERA

SERVES 6–8

generous 6$^1/_3$ cups chicken or vegetable stock

8 oz/225 g fresh thin asparagus spears

4 tbsp olive oil

6 oz/175 g young green beans, cut into 1-inch/2.5-cm lengths

6 oz/175 g young zucchini, quartered and cut into 1-inch/2.5-cm lengths

generous 1$^1/_2$ cups shelled fresh peas

1 onion, finely chopped

1–2 garlic cloves, finely chopped

generous 1$^5/_8$ cups risotto rice

4 scallions, cut into 1-inch/2.5-cm lengths

2 oz/55 g butter

1 cup freshly grated Parmesan cheese

2 tbsp snipped fresh chives

2 tbsp shredded fresh basil

salt and pepper

scallions, to garnish (optional)

Bring the stock to a boil in a pan, then reduce the heat and keep simmering gently over low heat while you are cooking the risotto.

Trim the woody ends of the asparagus and cut off the tips. Cut the stems into 1-inch/2.5-cm pieces and set aside with the tips.

Heat 2 tablespoons of the oil in a large skillet over high heat until very hot. Add the asparagus, beans, zucchini, and peas and stir-fry for 3–4 minutes until they are bright green and just starting to soften. Set aside.

Heat the remaining oil in a large, heavy-bottom pan over medium heat. Add the onion and cook, stirring occasionally, for 3 minutes, or until it starts to soften. Stir in the garlic and cook, while stirring, for 30 seconds.

Reduce the heat, add the rice, and mix to coat in oil. Cook, stirring constantly, for 2–3 minutes, or until the grains are translucent.

Gradually add the hot stock, a ladleful at a time. Stir constantly and add more liquid as the rice absorbs each addition. Increase the heat to medium so that the liquid bubbles. Cook for 20 minutes, or until all but 2 tablespoons of the liquid is absorbed and the rice is creamy.

Stir in the stir-fried vegetables, onion mixture, and scallions with the remaining stock. Cook for 2 minutes, stirring frequently, then season to taste with salt and pepper. Stir in the butter, Parmesan, chives, and basil.

Remove the pan from the heat. Transfer the risotto to a warmed serving dish, garnish with scallions, if liked, and serve at once.

THIS IS A DELICIOUS WAY TO USE THOSE FIRST GREEN VEGETABLES THAT SIGNAL THE ARRIVAL OF SPRING (LA PRIMAVERA IN ITALIAN). FEEL FREE TO ADD OTHER SEASONAL VEGETABLES.

MINTED GREEN RISOTTO

SERVES 6

4 cups chicken or
vegetable stock

2 tbsp butter

generous 1¹/₂ cups
shelled fresh peas or
thawed frozen peas

5⁵/₈ cups fresh
young spinach leaves,
washed and drained

1 bunch of fresh mint,
leaves stripped from stalks

2 tbsp chopped fresh basil

2 tbsp chopped
fresh oregano

pinch of freshly grated
nutmeg

4 tbsp mascarpone cheese
or heavy cream

2 tbsp vegetable oil

1 onion, finely chopped

2 celery stalks, including
leaves, finely chopped

2 garlic cloves,
finely chopped

¹/₂ tsp dried thyme

scant 1¹/₂ cups risotto rice

¹/₄ cup dry
white vermouth

³/₄ cup freshly grated
Parmesan cheese

Bring the stock to a boil in a pan, then reduce the heat and keep simmering gently over low heat while you are cooking the risotto.

Heat half the butter in a deep skillet over medium-high heat until sizzling. Add the peas, spinach, mint leaves, basil, and oregano and season with the nutmeg. Cook, stirring frequently, for 3 minutes, or until the spinach and mint leaves are wilted. Let cool slightly.

Pour the spinach mixture into a food processor and process for 15 seconds. Add the mascarpone (or cream) and process again for 1 minute. Transfer to a bowl and set aside.

Heat the oil and remaining butter in a large, heavy-bottom pan over medium heat. Add the onion, celery, garlic, and thyme and cook, stirring occasionally, for 2 minutes, or until the vegetables are softened.

Reduce the heat, add the rice, and mix to coat in oil and butter. Cook, stirring constantly, for 2–3 minutes, or until the grains are translucent.

Add the vermouth and cook, stirring constantly, until it has reduced.

Gradually add the hot stock, a ladleful at a time. Stir constantly and add more liquid as the rice absorbs each addition. Increase the heat to medium so that the liquid bubbles. Cook for 20 minutes, or until the liquid is absorbed and the rice is creamy.

Stir in the spinach-mascarpone mixture and the Parmesan. Transfer to warmed plates and serve at once.

THIS TASTY RISOTTO GETS ITS VIBRANT GREEN COLOR FROM THE SPINACH AND MINT. SERVE WITH ITALIAN-STYLE RUSTIC BREAD AND SALAD FOR AN INFORMAL SUPPER.

RADICCHIO RISOTTO

SERVES 6–8

1 large head radicchio,
outer damaged leaves
removed

generous 6¹/₃ cups
chicken or vegetable stock

2 tbsp corn or other
vegetable oil

2 tbsp butter

4 oz/115 g pancetta
or thick-cut smoked
bacon, diced

1 large onion,
finely chopped

1 garlic clove,
finely chopped

scant 2 cups risotto rice

¹/₄ cup heavy cream

¹/₂ cup freshly grated
Parmesan cheese

3–4 tbsp chopped fresh
flat-leaf parsley

salt and pepper

Cut the radicchio head in half lengthwise and remove the triangular core. Place the halves cut-side down and shred finely. Set aside.

Bring the stock to a boil in a pan, then reduce the heat and keep simmering gently over low heat while you are cooking the risotto.

Heat the oil and butter in a large, heavy-bottom pan over medium heat. Add the pancetta and cook, stirring occasionally, for 3–4 minutes until it starts to color. Add the onion and garlic and cook for 1 minute.

Reduce the heat, add the rice, and mix to coat in oil and butter. Cook, stirring constantly, for 2–3 minutes or until the grains are translucent. Add the radicchio and cook, stirring for 1 minute until it just starts to wilt.

Gradually add the hot stock, a ladleful at a time. Stir constantly and add more liquid as the rice absorbs each addition. Increase the heat to medium so that the liquid bubbles. Cook for 20 minutes, or until all the liquid is absorbed and the rice is creamy.

Stir in the cream, Parmesan, and parsley and season to taste with salt and pepper. Remove the pan from the heat and spoon the risotto onto warmed plates. Serve at once.

THE SLIGHTLY BITTER FLAVOR OF RADICCHIO IS BALANCED BY THE ADDITION OF SWEET HEAVY CREAM, WHILE PANCETTA PROVIDES A DELIGHTFUL SMOKY CONTRAST.

ASPARAGUS AND
SUN-DRIED TOMATO RISOTTO

SERVES 4

4 cups vegetable stock

1 tbsp olive oil

3 tbsp butter

1 small onion, finely chopped

6 sun-dried tomatoes, thinly sliced

generous 1³/₈ cups risotto rice

²/₃ cup dry white wine

8 oz/225 g fresh asparagus spears, cooked

³/₄ cup freshly grated Parmesan or Grana Padano cheese

salt and pepper

thinly pared lemon rind, to garnish

Bring the stock to a boil in a pan, then reduce the heat and keep simmering gently over low heat while you are cooking the risotto.

Heat the oil with 2 tablespoons of the butter in a deep pan over medium heat until the butter has melted. Stir in the onion and sun-dried tomatoes, and cook, stirring occasionally, for 5 minutes until the onion is soft and starting to turn golden. Do not brown.

Reduce the heat, add the rice, and mix to coat in oil and butter. Cook, stirring constantly, for 2–3 minutes, or until the grains are translucent.

Add the wine and cook, stirring constantly, until it has reduced.

Gradually add the hot stock, a ladleful at a time. Stir constantly and add more liquid as the rice absorbs each addition. Increase the heat to medium so that the liquid bubbles. Cook for 20 minutes, or until all the liquid is absorbed and the rice is creamy. Season to taste.

While the risotto is cooking, cut most of the asparagus into pieces about 1 inch/2.5 cm long. Keep several spears whole for garnishing the finished dish. Carefully fold the cut pieces of asparagus into the risotto for the last 5 minutes of cooking time.

Remove the risotto from the heat and add the remaining butter. Mix well, then stir in the Parmesan until it melts. Spoon the risotto onto individual warmed serving dishes and garnish with whole spears of asparagus. Sprinkle the lemon rind on top and serve.

IF USING SUN-DRIED TOMATOES IN OIL, SIMPLY DRAIN THEM WELL BEFORE SLICING. SUN-DRIED TOMATOES FROM A PACKAGE MUST FIRST BE SOAKED IN BOILING WATER UNTIL THEY ARE SOFT.

OVEN-BAKED RISOTTO WITH MUSHROOMS

SERVES 4

generous 5¹/₂ cups
chicken or vegetable stock

4 tbsp olive oil

14 oz/400 g portobello
mushrooms, thickly sliced

4 oz/115 g pancetta
or thick-cut smoked
bacon, diced

1 large onion,
finely chopped

2 garlic cloves,
finely chopped

generous 1⁵/₈ cups
risotto rice

2 tbsp chopped fresh
tarragon or
flat-leaf parsley

³/4 cup freshly grated
Parmesan cheese, plus
extra for sprinkling

salt and pepper

Preheat the oven to 350°F/180°C. Bring the stock to a boil in a pan, then reduce the heat and keep simmering gently over low heat while you are cooking the risotto.

Heat half the oil in a large, heavy-bottom skillet over high heat. Add the mushrooms and stir-fry for 2–3 minutes until golden and tender-crisp. Transfer to a plate.

Add the pancetta to the skillet and cook, stirring frequently, for 2 minutes, or until crisp and golden. Remove with a slotted spoon and add to the mushrooms on the plate.

Heat the remaining oil in a large, heavy-bottom pan over medium heat. Add the onion and cook, stirring occasionally, for 2 minutes. Add the garlic and cook for 1 minute.

Reduce the heat, add the rice, and mix to coat in oil. Cook, stirring constantly, for 2–3 minutes, or until the grains are translucent.

Gradually stir the hot stock into the rice, then add the mushroom and pancetta mixture and the tarragon. Season to taste with salt and pepper. Bring to a boil.

Remove the pan from the heat and transfer the mixture to a casserole or an ovenproof dish.

Cover and bake in the oven for 20 minutes, or until the rice is almost tender and most of the liquid is absorbed. Uncover and stir in the Parmesan. Continue to bake for an additional 15 minutes until the rice is creamy. Serve at once with extra Parmesan for sprinkling.

THIS EASY-TO-MAKE RISOTTO IS A GOOD CHOICE FOR ENTERTAINING BECAUSE IT ELIMINATES THE NEED FOR CONSTANT STIRRING.

RISOTTO WITH ARTICHOKE HEARTS

SERVES 4

8 oz/225 g canned artichoke hearts

5 cups chicken or vegetable stock

1 tbsp olive oil

3 tbsp butter

1 small onion, finely chopped

generous 1 3/8 cups risotto rice

3/4 cup freshly grated Parmesan or Grana Padano cheese

salt and pepper

fresh flat-leaf parsley sprigs, to garnish

Drain the artichoke hearts, reserving the liquid, and cut them into quarters.

Bring the stock to a boil in a pan, then reduce the heat and keep simmering gently over low heat while you are cooking the risotto.

Heat the oil with 2 tablespoons of the butter in a deep pan over medium heat until the butter has melted. Stir in the onion and cook gently, stirring occasionally, for 5 minutes, or until soft and starting to turn golden. Do not brown.

Add the rice and mix to coat in oil and butter. Cook, stirring constantly, for 2–3 minutes, or until the grains are translucent.

Gradually add the artichoke liquid and the hot stock, a ladle at a time. Stir constantly and add more liquid as the rice absorbs each addition. Increase the heat to medium so that the liquid bubbles. Cook for 15 minutes, then add the artichoke hearts. Cook for an additional 5 minutes, or until all the liquid is absorbed and the rice is creamy. Season to taste.

Remove the risotto from the heat and add the remaining butter. Mix well, then stir in the Parmesan until it melts. Season, if necessary. Spoon the risotto into warmed bowls, garnish with parsley sprigs, and serve at once.

As the can juices from the artichoke hearts are reserved and added to the rice, you may not need to use all the stock.

KIDNEY BEAN RISOTTO

SERVES 4

4 tbsp olive oil

1 onion, chopped

2 garlic cloves,
finely chopped

generous ³/4 cup
brown rice

2¹/2 cups vegetable stock

1 red bell pepper, seeded
and chopped

2 celery stalks, sliced

8 oz/225 g cremini
mushrooms, thinly sliced

15 oz/425 g canned red
kidney beans, drained
and rinsed

3 tbsp chopped fresh
parsley, plus extra
to garnish

scant ³/8 cup cashews

salt and pepper

Heat half the oil in a large, heavy-bottom pan. Add the onion and cook, stirring occasionally, for 5 minutes, or until softened. Add half the garlic and cook, stirring frequently, for 2 minutes, then add the rice and stir for 1 minute, or until the grains are thoroughly coated with the oil.

Add the stock and a pinch of salt and bring to a boil, stirring constantly. Reduce the heat, cover, and let simmer for 35–40 minutes, or until all the liquid has been absorbed.

Meanwhile, heat the remaining oil in a heavy-bottom skillet. Add the bell pepper and celery and cook, stirring frequently, for 5 minutes. Add the sliced mushrooms and the remaining garlic and cook, stirring frequently, for 4–5 minutes.

Stir the rice into the skillet. Add the beans, parsley, and cashews. Season to taste with salt and pepper and cook, stirring constantly, until hot. Transfer to a warmed serving dish, sprinkle with extra parsley, and serve at once.

You could also make this dish with a mixture of long-grain rice and wild rice instead of the brown rice. Follow the package instructions for cooking.

RISOTTO WITH ROASTED VEGETABLES

SERVES 4

5 cups chicken or vegetable stock

1 tbsp olive oil

3 tbsp butter

1 small onion, finely chopped

generous 1 3/8 cups risotto rice

8 oz/225 g roasted vegetables, such as bell peppers, zucchini, and eggplant, cut into chunks

3/4 cup freshly grated Parmesan or Grana Padano cheese

salt and pepper

2 tbsp finely chopped fresh herbs, to garnish

Bring the stock to a boil in a pan, then reduce the heat and keep simmering gently over low heat while you are cooking the risotto.

Heat the oil with 2 tablespoons of the butter in a deep pan over medium heat until the butter has melted. Add the onion and cook, stirring occasionally, for 5 minutes, until soft and starting to turn golden. Do not brown.

Reduce the heat, add the rice, and mix to coat in oil and butter. Cook, stirring constantly, for 2–3 minutes, or until the grains are translucent.

Gradually add the hot stock, a ladleful at a time. Stir constantly and add more liquid as the rice absorbs each addition. Increase the heat to medium so that the liquid bubbles. Cook for 15 minutes, then add most of the roasted vegetables, setting aside a few pieces to use as a garnish. Cook for an additional 5 minutes, or until all the liquid is absorbed and the rice is creamy. Season to taste with salt and pepper.

Remove the risotto from the heat and add the remaining butter. Mix well, then stir in the Parmesan until it melts. Spoon the risotto onto warmed individual plates, arrange vegetables around it or on top to garnish, and then sprinkle with fresh herbs before serving at once.

ROASTED MEDITERRANEAN VEGETABLES HAVE A DELICIOUSLY SWEET FLAVOR. TO PREPARE THEM, PLACE THE RAW VEGETABLES IN AN OILED ROASTING PAN AND COOK IN THE OVEN AT 400°F/200°C FOR 20–25 MINUTES.

WILD MUSHROOM RISOTTO

SERVES 6

1/2 cup dried porcini or morel mushrooms

5 cups chicken or vegetable stock

about 1 lb 2 oz/500 g mixed fresh wild mushrooms, such as porcini, horse mushrooms, and chanterelles, halved if large

4 tbsp olive oil

3–4 garlic cloves, finely chopped

2 oz/55 g butter

1 onion, finely chopped

generous 1 5/8 cups risotto rice

1/4 cup dry white vermouth

1 cup freshly grated Parmesan cheese

4 tbsp chopped fresh flat-leaf parsley

salt and pepper

Place the dried mushrooms in a heatproof bowl and add boiling water to cover. Set aside to soak for 30 minutes, then carefully lift out and pat dry. Strain the soaking liquid through a strainer lined with paper towels and set aside.

Bring the stock to a boil in a pan, then reduce the heat and keep simmering gently over low heat while you are cooking the risotto.

Trim the fresh mushrooms and gently brush clean. Heat 3 tablespoons of the oil in a large skillet. Add the fresh mushrooms and stir-fry for 1–2 minutes. Add the garlic and the soaked mushrooms and cook, stirring frequently, for 2 minutes. Transfer to a plate.

Heat the remaining oil and half the butter in a large, heavy-bottom pan. Add the onion and cook over medium heat, stirring occasionally, for 2 minutes, until softened.

Reduce the heat, add the rice, and mix to coat in oil and butter. Cook, stirring constantly, for 2–3 minutes, or until the grains are translucent.

Add the vermouth and cook, stirring constantly, for 1 minute until reduced.

Gradually add the hot stock, a ladleful at a time. Stir constantly and add more liquid as the rice absorbs each addition. Increase the heat to medium so that the liquid bubbles. Cook for 20 minutes, or until all the liquid is absorbed and the rice is creamy.

Add half the reserved mushroom soaking liquid to the risotto and stir in the mushrooms. Season to taste with salt and pepper and add more mushroom liquid, if necessary. Remove the pan from the heat and stir in the remaining butter, the grated Parmesan, and chopped parsley. Serve at once.

DISTINCTIVE-TASTING WILD MUSHROOMS, SO POPULAR IN ITALY, GIVE THIS AROMATIC RISOTTO A WONDERFUL, ROBUST FLAVOR.

The main rice-growing regions of Italy are in the north, which also boasts many of the country's most famous ports. So it is hardly surprising that some of the most delicious risotti are made with fish and seafood. The city of Venice has a reputation for magnificent fish dishes and likes to claim that it also invented risotto. While this may be debatable, there is certainly no question mark over the fabulous Venetian Seafood Risotto.

Many of the recipes in this chapter are perfect for dinner parties, yet there are also equally tasty but less extravagant dishes that would make an ideal family supper. Even canned tuna makes a surprising appearance in a flavorsome combination with tomatoes and fresh herbs.

It's always best to buy fish and seafood on the day you are planning to cook and eat it and, in general, fresh is best because the texture and flavor are both at their peak. However, many types of fish do freeze well, but make sure that

PART THREE
THE FISHERMAN'S CATCH

they are thoroughly thawed before you start cooking. Frozen seafood isn't so successful, although sometimes that may be all that is easily available. Shellfish, such as mussels, are invariably best when bought live and then cooked shortly before serving.

Although a homemade fish stock is packed with subtle flavor and recommended for authentic fish risotti, many people find it a chore to make. It's also quite a messy and smelly business. Ready-made varieties are available, but equally, you can simply substitute chicken stock without damaging the delicate flavor of the finished dish.

BLACK RISOTTO

SERVES 6

4 cups fish or chicken stock, simmering

2–3 tbsp olive oil

1 lb/450 g cleaned raw squid or cuttlefish, cut crosswise into thin strips, rinsed and patted dry

2 tbsp lemon juice

2 tbsp butter

3–4 garlic cloves, finely chopped

1 tsp crushed dried chili, or to taste

generous 1⅝ cups risotto rice

½ cup dry white wine

2 sachets squid or cuttlefish ink

2 tbsp chopped fresh flat-leaf parsley

salt and pepper

Bring the stock to a boil in a pan, then reduce the heat and keep it simmering gently over low heat while you are cooking the risotto.

Heat half the olive oil in a large, heavy-bottom skillet over medium-high heat. When the oil is very hot, add the squid strips and stir-fry for 2–3 minutes until just cooked. Transfer to a plate and sprinkle with the lemon juice.

Heat the remaining oil and butter in a large, heavy-bottom pan over medium heat. Add the garlic and chili and cook gently for 1 minute.

Reduce the heat, add the rice, and mix to coat in oil and butter. Cook, stirring constantly, for 2–3 minutes, or until the grains are translucent.

Pour in the wine and cook, stirring constantly, for 1 minute until reduced.

Gradually add the hot stock, a ladleful at a time. Stir constantly and add more liquid as the rice absorbs each addition. Increase the heat to medium so that the liquid bubbles. Cook for 20 minutes, or until all the liquid is absorbed and the rice is creamy.

Just before adding the last ladleful of stock, add the squid ink to the stock and stir to blend completely. Stir into the risotto with the reserved squid pieces and the parsley. Season to taste with salt and pepper.

Serve at once.

MAKE SURE THAT THE OIL IS VERY HOT BEFORE YOU ADD THE STRIPS OF SQUID TO THE PAN. COOK IT QUICKLY, STIRRING CONSTANTLY. OVERCOOKED SQUID WILL BE TOUGH AND INEDIBLE.

SAFFRON AND LEMON RISOTTO WITH SCALLOPS

SERVES 4

16 live scallops, shucked

juice of 1 lemon, plus extra for seasoning

5 cups fish or vegetable stock

1 tbsp olive oil, plus extra for brushing

3 tbsp butter

1 small onion, finely chopped

generous 1³/₈ cups risotto rice

1 tsp crumbled saffron threads

2 tbsp vegetable oil

1 cup freshly grated Parmesan or Grana Padano cheese

salt and pepper

To garnish

1 lemon, cut into wedges

2 tsp grated lemon zest

Place the scallops in a nonmetallic bowl and mix with the lemon juice. Cover the bowl with plastic wrap and let chill in the refrigerator for 15 minutes.

Bring the stock to a boil in a pan, then reduce the heat and keep simmering gently over low heat while you are cooking the risotto.

Heat the oil with 2 tablespoons of the butter in a deep pan over medium heat until the butter has melted. Add the onion and cook, stirring occasionally, for 5 minutes, or until soft and starting to turn golden. Do not brown.

Add the rice and mix to coat in oil and butter. Cook, stirring constantly, for 2–3 minutes, or until the grains are translucent. Dissolve the saffron in 4 tablespoons of hot stock and add to the rice.

Gradually add the remaining stock, a ladleful at a time. Stir constantly and add more liquid as the rice absorbs each addition. Increase the heat to medium so that the liquid bubbles. Cook for 20 minutes, or until all the liquid is absorbed and the rice is creamy. Season to taste.

When the risotto is nearly cooked, preheat a grill pan over high heat. Brush the scallops with oil and sear on the grill pan for 3–4 minutes on each side, depending on their thickness. Take care not to overcook or they will be rubbery.

Remove the risotto from the heat and add the remaining butter. Mix well, then stir in the Parmesan until it melts. Season with lemon juice, adding just 1 teaspoon at a time and tasting as you go.

Place a large scoop of risotto on each of 4 warmed plates. Arrange 4 scallops and lemon wedges around it, sprinkle with lemon zest, and serve at once.

THIS DISH IS BEST MADE WITH FRESH SCALLOPS. THEY ARE WIDELY AVAILABLE ON THE HALF SHELL. IF YOU HAVE TO USE FROZEN SCALLOPS, MAKE SURE THAT THEY ARE COMPLETELY THAWED FIRST.

GENOESE SEAFOOD RISOTTO

SERVES 4

generous 5¹/₂ cups fish or chicken stock

3 tbsp olive oil

9 oz/250 g mixed seafood, preferably raw or live, such as shrimp, squid, mussels, and clams, prepared as necessary

2 tbsp chopped fresh oregano, plus extra to garnish

2 oz/55 g butter

2 garlic cloves, chopped

generous 1⁵/₈ cups risotto rice

¹/₂ cup freshly grated romano or Parmesan cheese

salt and pepper

Bring the stock to a boil in a pan, then reduce the heat and keep simmering gently over low heat while you are cooking the risotto.

Heat 2 tablespoons of the oil in a large skillet and add the raw or live mixed seafood. Cook over medium-high heat, stirring frequently, for 5 minutes. If the seafood is already cooked, stir-fry for 2 minutes. Remove the skillet from the heat and stir in the oregano.

Heat the remaining oil with 2 tablespoons of the butter in a deep pan over medium heat until the butter has melted. Add the garlic and cook, stirring, for 1 minute.

Reduce the heat, add the rice, and mix to coat in oil and butter. Cook, stirring constantly, for 2–3 minutes, or until the grains are translucent.

Gradually add the hot stock, a ladleful at a time. Stir constantly and add more liquid as the rice absorbs each addition. Increase the heat to medium so that the liquid bubbles. Cook for 20 minutes, or until all the liquid is absorbed and the rice is creamy.

About 5 minutes before the rice is ready, add the seafood to the pan and mix well.

Remove the pan from the heat and season to taste. Add the remaining butter and mix well, then stir in the grated cheese until it melts. Spoon onto warmed plates and serve at once, garnished with extra oregano.

THE GENOESE ARE EXCELLENT COOKS, AND THEY MAKE PARTICULARLY DELICIOUS FISH DISHES FLAVORED WITH THE LOCAL OLIVE OIL.

RISOTTO WITH
SQUID AND GARLIC BUTTER

SERVES 4

8–12 raw baby squid

5 cups fish or
chicken stock

1 tbsp olive oil

5 1/2 oz/150 g butter

1 small onion,
finely chopped

generous 1 3/8 cups
risotto rice

3 garlic cloves, crushed

3/4 cup freshly grated
Parmesan or Grana
Padano cheese

salt and pepper

2 tbsp finely chopped
fresh parsley, to garnish

Clean the squid, carefully removing and discarding the innards and the membrane lining. Rinse well and pat dry. Dice the larger tentacles. Cut the squid in half lengthwise, then score with a sharp knife, making horizontal and vertical cuts.

Bring the stock to a boil in a pan, then reduce the heat and keep simmering gently over low heat while you are cooking the risotto.

Heat the oil with 2 tablespoons of the butter in a deep pan over medium heat until the butter has melted. Stir in the onion and cook, stirring occasionally, for 5 minutes, or until soft and starting to turn golden. Do not brown.

Add the rice and mix to coat in oil and butter. Cook, stirring constantly, for 2–3 minutes, or until the grains are translucent.

Gradually add the hot stock, a ladleful at a time. Stir constantly and add more liquid as the rice absorbs each addition. Increase the heat to medium so that the liquid bubbles. Cook for 20 minutes, or until all the liquid is absorbed and the rice is creamy. Season to taste.

When the risotto is nearly cooked, melt 4 oz/115 g of the remaining butter in a heavy-bottom skillet. Add the garlic and cook over low heat for 2 minutes, or until soft.

Increase the heat to high, add the squid, and toss to cook. Do this for no more than 2–3 minutes or the squid will become tough. Remove the squid from the skillet, draining carefully and reserving the garlic butter.

Remove the risotto from the heat and add the remaining butter. Mix well, then stir in the Parmesan until it melts. Spoon the risotto onto warmed serving plates and arrange the squid on top. Spoon some of the garlic butter over each portion. Sprinkle with the chopped parsley and serve at once.

TO CLEAN SQUID, PULL THE HEAD AND BODY APART. THE INNARDS WILL COME AWAY WITH THE HEAD. CUT OFF THE TENTACLES AND SQUEEZE OUT THE BEAK. PULL OUT THE QUILL FROM THE BODY. RUB OFF THE SKIN UNDER COLD RUNNING WATER AND PAT THE BODY SAC DRY.

SHRIMP AND ASPARAGUS RISOTTO

SERVES 4

5 cups vegetable stock

12 oz/375 g fresh
asparagus spears, cut into
2-inch/5-cm lengths

2 tbsp olive oil

1 onion, finely chopped

1 garlic clove,
finely chopped

generous 1⅝ cups
risotto rice

1 lb/450 g raw jumbo
shrimp, shelled
and deveined

2 tbsp olive paste
or tapenade

2 tbsp chopped fresh basil

salt and pepper

To garnish

fresh Parmesan cheese

fresh basil sprigs

Bring the stock to a boil in a large pan. Add the asparagus and cook for 3 minutes until just tender. Strain, reserving the stock, and refresh the asparagus under cold running water. Drain and set aside.

Return the stock to the pan and keep simmering gently over low heat while you are cooking the risotto.

Heat the olive oil in a large, heavy-bottom pan. Add the onion and cook over medium heat, stirring occasionally, for 5 minutes until softened. Add the garlic and cook for an additional 30 seconds.

Reduce the heat, add the rice, and mix to coat in oil. Cook, stirring constantly, for 2–3 minutes, or until the grains are translucent.

Gradually add the hot stock, a ladleful at a time. Stir constantly and add more liquid as the rice absorbs each addition. Increase the heat to medium so that the liquid bubbles. Cook for 20 minutes, until all the liquid is absorbed and the rice is creamy. Add the shrimp and asparagus with the last ladleful of stock.

Remove the pan from the heat, stir in the olive paste and basil, and season to taste with salt and pepper. Spoon the risotto onto warmed plates and serve at once, garnished with Parmesan cheese and basil sprigs.

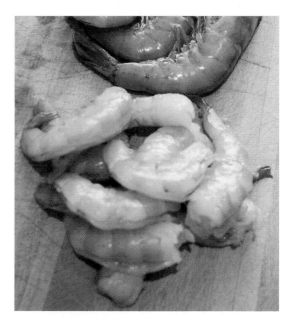

AN UNUSUAL AND STRIKING
DISH WITH FRESH SHRIMP AND
ASPARAGUS IS VERY SIMPLE TO
PREPARE AND IDEAL FOR
IMPROMPTU SUPPER PARTIES.

RISOTTO WITH CLAMS

SERVES 6

1/4 cup olive oil

1 large onion, finely chopped

4 lb 8 oz/2 kg tiny clams, such as Venus, well scrubbed

1/2 cup dry white wine

4 cups fish stock

2 1/2 cups water

3 garlic cloves, finely chopped

1/2 tsp crushed dried chili

scant 2 cups risotto rice

3 ripe plum tomatoes, peeled and coarsely chopped

3 tbsp lemon juice

2 tbsp chopped fresh chervil or parsley

salt and pepper

THIS SIMPLE RECIPE IS AN EXCELLENT WAY OF USING THE TINY VENUS CLAMS WHEN THEY ARE IN SEASON. THE TOMATOES ADD A SPLASH OF COLOR.

Heat 1–2 tablespoons of the oil in a large, heavy-bottom pan over medium-high heat. Add the onion and cook, stirring constantly, for 1 minute. Add the clams and wine and cover tightly. Cook, shaking the pan frequently, for 2–3 minutes until the clams start to open. Remove from the heat and discard any clams that do not open.

When cool enough to handle, remove the clams from their shells. Rinse in the cooking liquid. Cover the clams and set aside. Strain the cooking liquid through a coffee filter or a strainer lined with paper towels and set aside.

Bring the stock and water to a boil in a pan, then reduce the heat and keep simmering gently over low heat while you are cooking the risotto.

Heat the remaining oil in a large, heavy-bottom pan over medium heat. Add the garlic and chili and cook gently for 1 minute.

Reduce the heat, add the rice, and mix to coat in oil. Cook, stirring constantly, for 2–3 minutes, or until the grains are translucent.

Gradually add the hot stock mixture, a ladleful at a time. Stir constantly and add more liquid as the rice absorbs each addition. Increase the heat to medium so that the liquid bubbles. Cook for 20 minutes, or until all the liquid is absorbed and the rice is creamy.

Stir in the tomatoes, reserved clams and their cooking liquid, the lemon juice, and chervil. Heat through gently. Season to taste with salt and pepper. Spoon the risotto onto warmed plates and serve at once.

RISOTTO WITH SOLE AND TOMATOES

SERVES 4

5 cups fish or chicken stock

3 tbsp olive oil

3 tbsp butter

1 small onion, finely chopped

generous 1³/₈ cups risotto rice

1 lb/450 g tomatoes, peeled, seeded, and cut into strips

6 sun-dried tomatoes in olive oil, drained and thinly sliced

3 tbsp tomato paste

¹/₄ cup red wine

1 lb/450 g sole or flounder fillets, skinned

1 cup freshly grated Parmesan or Grana Padano cheese

salt and pepper

2 tbsp finely chopped fresh cilantro, to garnish

Bring the stock to a boil in a pan, then reduce the heat and keep simmering gently over low heat while you are cooking the risotto.

Heat 1 tablespoon of the oil with 2 tablespoons of the butter in a deep pan over medium heat until the butter has melted. Stir in the onion and cook, stirring occasionally, for 5 minutes, or until soft and starting to turn golden. Do not brown.

Reduce the heat, add the rice, and mix to coat in oil and butter. Cook, stirring constantly, for 2–3 minutes, or until the grains are translucent.

Gradually add the hot stock, a ladleful at a time. Stir constantly and add more liquid as the rice absorbs each addition. Increase the heat to medium so that the liquid bubbles. Cook for 20 minutes, or until all the liquid is absorbed and the rice is creamy. Season to taste.

While the risotto is cooking, heat the remaining oil in a large, heavy-bottom skillet. Add the fresh and dried tomatoes. Stir well and cook over medium heat for 10–15 minutes, or until soft and slushy.

Stir in the tomato paste and wine. Bring the sauce to a boil, then reduce the heat until it is just simmering.

Cut the fish into strips and add to the sauce. Stir gently. Cook for 5 minutes, or until the fish flakes when checked with a fork. Most of the

liquid should be absorbed, but if it isn't, remove the fish and then increase the heat to reduce the sauce.

Remove the risotto from the heat when all the liquid has been absorbed and add the remaining butter. Mix well, then stir in the Parmesan until it melts.

Place the risotto on serving plates and arrange the fish and sauce on top. Garnish with fresh cilantro and serve at once.

To skin a flat fish fillet, place it on a board, tail end toward you. Make a small cut through the skin, then, gripping the tail end in one hand, pull off the skin toward the head end with the other hand.

VENETIAN SEAFOOD RISOTTO

SERVES 4

8 oz/225 g raw shrimp

2 garlic cloves, halved

1 lemon, sliced

8 oz/225 g live mussels, scrubbed and debearded

8 oz/225 g live clams, scrubbed

2½ cups water

4 oz/115 g butter

1 tbsp olive oil

1 onion, finely chopped

2 tbsp chopped fresh flat-leaf parsley

generous 1⅝ cups risotto rice

½ cup dry white wine

8 oz/225 g cleaned raw squid, cut into small pieces, or squid rings

4 tbsp Marsala

salt and pepper

Shell the shrimp, reserving the head and shells. Cut a slit along the back of each and remove the dark vein. Wrap the heads and shells in a square of cheesecloth and pound with a pestle or a rolling pin, reserving any liquid they yield.

Place the garlic, lemon, mussels, and clams in a pan and add the wrapped shells and any reserved liquid. Pour in the water, cover tightly, and bring to a boil over high heat. Cook, shaking the pan frequently, for 5 minutes until the shellfish have opened. Discard any that stay closed. When cool enough to handle, remove the clams and mussels from their shells and put in a bowl. Strain the cooking liquid through a cheesecloth-lined strainer into a measuring cup. Make up the amount of liquid to 5 cups with water.

Pour this liquid into a pan. Bring to a boil, then reduce the heat and keep simmering gently over low heat while you make the risotto.

Melt 2 tablespoons of the butter with the olive oil in a deep pan. Add the onion and half the parsley and cook over medium heat, stirring occasionally, for 5 minutes, or until softened.

Reduce the heat, add the rice, and mix to coat in oil and butter. Cook, stirring constantly, for 2–3 minutes, or until the grains are translucent.

Add the wine and cook, stirring constantly, for 1 minute until reduced.

Gradually add the hot stock, a ladleful at a time. Stir constantly and add more liquid as the rice absorbs each addition. Increase the heat to medium so that the liquid bubbles. Cook for 20 minutes, or until all the liquid is absorbed and the rice is creamy.

About 5 minutes before the rice is ready, melt 2 oz/55 g of the remaining butter in a heavy-bottom pan. Add the squid and cook, stirring frequently, for 3 minutes, then add the reserved shrimp and cook for an additional 2–3 minutes, until the squid is opaque and the shrimp have changed color. Stir in the Marsala, bring to a boil, and cook until all the liquid has evaporated.

Stir the squid, shrimp, mussels, and clams into the rice, add the remaining butter and parsley, and season to taste with salt and pepper. Heat through briefly and serve at once.

WHEN PREPARING LIVE SHELLFISH, ALWAYS DISCARD ANY WITH DAMAGED SHELLS OR THAT DO NOT CLOSE IMMEDIATELY WHEN TAPPED SHARPLY WITH A KNIFE.

RISOTTO WITH TUNA AND PINE NUTS

SERVES 4

5 cups fish or
chicken stock

4 tbsp olive oil

3 tbsp butter

1 small onion,
finely chopped

generous 1 3/8 cups
risotto rice

8 oz/225 g tuna, canned
and drained, or broiled
fresh steaks

8–10 black olives, pitted
and sliced

1 small pimiento,
thinly sliced

1 tsp finely chopped
fresh parsley

1 tsp finely chopped
fresh marjoram

2 tbsp white wine vinegar

3/8 cup pine nuts

1 garlic clove, chopped

8 oz/225 g fresh
tomatoes, peeled, seeded,
and diced

3/4 cup Parmesan or
Grana Padano cheese

salt and pepper

Bring the stock to a boil in a pan, then reduce the heat and keep simmering gently over low heat while you are cooking the risotto.

Heat 1 tablespoon of oil with 2 tablespoons of the butter in a deep pan over medium heat until the butter has melted. Add the onion and cook, stirring occasionally, for 5 minutes, or until soft and starting to turn golden. Do not brown.

Reduce the heat, add the rice, and mix to coat in oil and butter. Cook, stirring constantly, for 2–3 minutes, or until the grains are translucent.

Gradually add the stock, a ladleful at a time. Stir constantly and add more liquid as the rice absorbs each addition. Increase the heat to medium so that the liquid bubbles. Cook for 20 minutes until all the liquid is absorbed and the rice is creamy. Season to taste.

While the risotto is cooking, flake the tuna into a bowl and mix in the olives, pimiento, parsley, marjoram, and vinegar. Season to taste.

Heat the remaining oil in a small skillet over high heat. Add the pine nuts and garlic. Cook, stirring constantly, for 2 minutes, or until they just start to brown.

Add the tomatoes to the skillet and mix well. Continue cooking over medium heat for 3–4 minutes or until they are thoroughly warm.

Pour the tomato mixture over the tuna mixture and mix. Fold into the risotto 5 minutes before the end of the cooking time.

Remove the risotto from the heat when all the liquid has been absorbed and add the remaining butter. Mix well, then stir in the Parmesan until it melts. Serve at once.

COOK FRESH TUNA STEAKS UNDER A BROILER OR ON A GRILL PAN FOR A FEW MINUTES ON EACH SIDE. THE TUNA NEEDS TO FLAKE EASILY BUT NOT TO BE TOO WELL DONE.

The risotti in this chapter will be a revelation to passionate carnivores who think of rice dishes as somehow lacking and unsatisfying, and their versatility will delight everyone who relishes variety in their diet.

These modern risotti differ from their more traditional counterparts in that the meat is often cooked separately from the rice and other flavorings. Purists may sneer, arguing that the risotto is then reduced to being a mere accompaniment—a distinctly un-Italian way to serve it. This is easily countered by the well-known tradition of serving Risotto Milanese with the famous veal stew, osso buco.

The reasons for cooking the meat separately are very simple. Frequently, it requires a far longer cooking time than the rice. Also, if it is on the bone or in larger pieces, it would be quite difficult to stir the risotto constantly and thoroughly while the stock is ladled into the pan.

PART FOUR
RISOTTO CON CARNE

Of course, this is not invariably the case and fabulous risotti with diced chicken or sliced ham or sausage are made in the time-honored fashion.

A meat or chicken risotto provides a very substantial and nutritious meal, supplying a good balance of all food groups as well as essential vitamins and minerals. More to the point, perhaps, they taste superb and are as well-suited to family meals as they are to informal supper parties with friends. Whether your preference is for robust and spicy dishes or more subtle combinations of complementary flavors, there is sure to be the perfect risotto for you among the recipes in this chapter.

SPICY PORK RISOTTO

SERVES 4

1 thick slice white bread

water or milk, for soaking

1 lb/450 g fresh
ground pork

2 garlic cloves, minced

1 tbsp finely chopped onion

1 tsp black peppercorns,
lightly crushed

pinch of salt

1 egg

corn oil, for pan-frying

14 oz/400 g canned
chopped tomatoes

1 tbsp tomato paste

1 tsp dried oregano

1 tsp fennel seeds

pinch of sugar

4 cups beef stock

1 tbsp olive oil

3 tbsp butter

1 small onion,
finely chopped

generous 1³/₈ cups
risotto rice

²/₃ cup red wine

salt and pepper

fresh basil leaves, to garnish

Cut off and discard the crust from the bread, then soak in the water or milk for 5 minutes to soften. Drain and squeeze well to remove all the liquid. Mix the bread, pork, garlic, onion, crushed peppercorns, and salt together in a bowl. Add the egg and mix well.

Heat the corn oil in a skillet over medium heat. Form the meat mixture into balls and brown a few at a time in the oil. Remove from the skillet, drain, and set aside until all the meatballs are cooked.

Combine the tomatoes, tomato paste, oregano, fennel seeds, and sugar in a heavy-bottom pan. Add the meatballs. Bring the sauce to a boil over medium heat, then reduce the heat and let simmer for 30 minutes, or until the meat is thoroughly cooked.

To make the risotto, bring the stock to a boil in a pan, then reduce the heat and keep simmering gently over low heat while you are cooking the risotto.

Heat the olive oil with 2 tablespoons of the butter in a deep pan over medium heat until the butter has melted. Stir in the onion and cook, stirring occasionally, for 5 minutes, or until soft and starting to turn golden. Do not brown.

Reduce the heat, add the rice, and mix to coat in oil and butter. Cook, stirring constantly, for 2–3 minutes, or until the grains are translucent.

Add the wine and cook, stirring constantly, for 1 minute until reduced. Gradually add the hot stock, a ladleful at a time. Stir constantly and add more liquid as the rice absorbs each addition. Increase the heat to medium so that the liquid bubbles. Cook for 20 minutes, or until all the liquid is absorbed. Season to taste.

Lift out the cooked meatballs and add to the risotto. Remove the risotto from the heat and add the remaining butter. Mix well. Arrange the risotto and a few meatballs on plates. Drizzle with tomato sauce, garnish with basil, and serve.

FOR THE BEST QUALITY, IT'S ALWAYS BEST TO BUY A LEAN, SINGLE PIECE OF MEAT, TRIM OFF ANY FAT, AND THEN GRIND IT AT HOME—EITHER USING A TRADITIONAL GRINDER OR IN A FOOD PROCESSOR.

CHICKEN RISOTTO WITH SAFFRON

SERVES 4

generous 5¹/₂ cups
chicken stock

4¹/₂ oz/125 g butter

2 lb/900 g skinless,
boneless chicken breasts,
thinly sliced

1 large onion, chopped

1 lb 2 oz/500 g
risotto rice

²/₃ cup white wine

1 tsp crumbled saffron
threads

¹/₂ cup freshly grated
Parmesan cheese

salt and pepper

Bring the stock to a boil in a pan, then reduce the heat and keep simmering gently over low heat while you are cooking the risotto.

Meanwhile, heat 2 oz/55 g of the butter in a deep pan, and add the chicken and onion and cook, stirring frequently, for 8 minutes, or until golden brown.

Add the rice and mix to coat in the butter. Cook, stirring constantly for 2–3 minutes, or until the grains are translucent. Add the wine and cook, stirring constantly, for 1 minute until reduced.

Mix the saffron with 4 tablespoons of the hot stock. Add the liquid to the rice and cook, stirring constantly, until it is absorbed.

Gradually add the remaining hot stock, a ladleful at a time. Stir constantly and add more liquid as the rice absorbs each addition. Cook for 20 minutes, or until all the liquid is absorbed and the rice is creamy. Season to taste.

Remove the risotto from the heat and add the remaining butter. Mix well, then stir in the Parmesan until it melts. Spoon the risotto onto warmed plates and serve at once.

THE POSSIBILITIES FOR RISOTTO ARE ENDLESS— TRY ADDING THE FOLLOWING JUST AT THE END OF COOKING TIME: CASHEWS AND CORN, LIGHTLY SAUTÉED ZUCCHINI AND BASIL, OR ARTICHOKES AND OYSTER MUSHROOMS.

HOT PEPPER LAMB
IN RED WINE RISOTTO

SERVES 4

4 tbsp all-purpose flour

8 pieces neck of lamb or lamb chops

4 tbsp olive oil

1 green bell pepper, seeded and thinly sliced

1–2 fresh green chilies, seeded and thinly sliced

2 small onions, 1 thinly sliced and 1 finely chopped

2 garlic cloves, thinly sliced

2 tbsp torn fresh basil

1/2 cup red wine

4 tbsp red wine vinegar

8 cherry tomatoes

1/2 cup water

5 cups chicken stock

3 tbsp butter

generous 1 3/8 cups risotto rice

3/4 cup freshly grated Parmesan or Grana Padano cheese

salt and pepper

Mix the flour with salt and pepper to taste on a plate. Coat the lamb in the flour, shaking off any excess. Heat 3 tablespoons of the oil in a large ovenproof casserole over high heat. Add the lamb and cook until browned all over. Remove from the casserole and set aside.

Toss the bell pepper, chilies, sliced onion, garlic, and basil in the oil left in the casserole for 3 minutes, or until lightly browned. Add the wine and vinegar, bring to a boil, and continue cooking over high heat for 3–4 minutes until the liquid is reduced to 2 tablespoons.

Add the tomatoes and the water, stir, and bring to a boil. Return the meat, cover, and reduce the heat as low as possible. Cook for 30 minutes, or until the meat is tender, turning occasionally. Check occasionally and add 2–3 tablespoons of water if necessary.

To make the risotto, bring the stock to a boil in a pan, then reduce the heat and keep simmering gently over low heat while you are cooking the risotto.

Heat the remaining oil with 2 tablespoons of the butter in a deep pan over medium heat until the butter has melted. Add the chopped onion and cook, stirring occasionally, for 5 minutes, or until soft and starting to turn golden. Do not brown.

Reduce the heat, add the rice, and mix to coat in oil and butter. Cook, stirring constantly, for 2–3 minutes, or until the grains are translucent.

Gradually add the hot stock, a ladleful at a time. Stir constantly and add more liquid as the rice absorbs each addition. Increase the heat to medium so that the liquid bubbles. Cook for 20 minutes, or until all the liquid is absorbed and the rice is creamy. Season to taste.

Remove the risotto from the heat and add the remaining butter. Mix well, then stir in the Parmesan until it melts. Arrange a scoop of risotto on each plate and sprinkle with peppers and tomatoes. Top with the lamb and serve.

THE LAMB COOKS MOST EVENLY IF THE PIECES ARE ABOUT THE SAME THICKNESS AND THE CASSEROLE IS LARGE ENOUGH TO HOLD THEM IN A SINGLE LAYER.

SAUSAGE AND ROSEMARY RISOTTO

SERVES 4–6

2 long fresh rosemary sprigs, plus extra to garnish

generous 5 1/2 cups chicken stock

2 tbsp olive oil

2 oz/55 g butter

1 large onion, finely chopped

1 celery stalk, finely chopped

2 garlic cloves, finely chopped

1/2 tsp dried thyme leaves

1 lb/450 g pork sausage, such as luganega or Cumberland, cut into 1/2-inch/1-cm pieces

generous 1 5/8 cups risotto rice

1/2 cup fruity red wine

3/4 cup freshly grated Parmesan cheese

salt and pepper

A SPECIALTY OF NORTHERN ITALY, LUGANEGA IS A SLIGHTLY SPICY PORK SAUSAGE. IT IS USUALLY SOLD IN A CONTINUOUS COIL RATHER THAN IN SEPARATE LINKS.

Strip the long thin leaves from the rosemary sprigs and chop finely, then set aside.

Bring the stock to a boil in a pan, then reduce the heat and keep simmering gently over low heat while you are cooking the risotto.

Heat the oil and half the butter in a deep pan over medium heat. Add the onion and celery and cook, stirring occasionally, for 2 minutes. Stir in the garlic, thyme, sausage, and rosemary. Cook, stirring frequently, for 5 minutes, or until the sausage starts to brown. Transfer the sausage to a plate.

Reduce the heat, add the rice, and mix to coat in oil and butter. Cook, stirring constantly, for 2–3 minutes, or until the grains are translucent.

Add the wine and cook, stirring constantly, for 1 minute until reduced.

Gradually add the hot stock, a ladleful at a time. Stir constantly and add more liquid as the rice absorbs each addition. Increase the heat to medium so that the liquid bubbles. Cook for 20 minutes, or until all the liquid is absorbed and the rice is creamy.

Toward the end of cooking, return the sausage pieces to the risotto and heat through. Season to taste with salt and pepper.

Remove from the heat and add the remaining butter. Mix well, then stir in the Parmesan until it melts. Spoon the risotto onto warmed plates, garnish with rosemary sprigs, and serve.

RISOTTO WITH CHARGRILLED CHICKEN BREAST

SERVES 4

4 boneless chicken breasts, about 4 oz/115 g each

grated rind and juice of 1 lemon

5 tbsp olive oil

1 garlic clove, crushed

8 fresh thyme sprigs, finely chopped

4 cups chicken stock

3 tbsp butter

1 small onion, finely chopped

generous 1 3/8 cups risotto rice

2/3 cup dry white wine

3/4 cup freshly grated Parmesan or Grana Padano cheese

salt and pepper

To garnish

lemon wedges

fresh thyme sprigs

Place the chicken breasts in a shallow, nonmetallic dish and season. Mix the lemon rind and juice, 4 tablespoons of the olive oil, the garlic, and thyme together in a bowl. Spoon the mixture over the chicken and rub in. Cover with plastic wrap and let marinate in the refrigerator for 4–6 hours.

Remove the chicken from the refrigerator and return to room temperature. Preheat a grill pan over high heat. Put the chicken, skin-side down, on the grill pan and cook for 10 minutes, or until the skin is crisp and starting to brown. Turn over and brown the underside. Reduce the heat and cook for an additional 10–15 minutes, or until the juices run clear when pierced with a skewer.

Meanwhile, bring the stock to a boil in a pan, then reduce the heat and keep simmering gently over low heat while you are cooking the risotto.

Heat the remaining oil with 2 tablespoons of the butter in a deep pan over medium heat until the butter has melted. Add the onion and cook, stirring occasionally, for 5 minutes, or until soft and starting to turn golden. Do not brown.

Reduce the heat, add the rice, and mix to coat in oil and butter. Cook, stirring constantly, for 2–3 minutes, or until the grains are translucent.

Add the wine and cook, stirring constantly, for 1 minute until reduced.

Gradually add the hot stock, a ladleful at a time. Stir constantly and add more liquid as the rice absorbs each addition. Increase the heat to medium so that the liquid bubbles. Cook for 20 minutes, or until all the liquid is absorbed and the rice is creamy. Season to taste.

Transfer the cooked chicken to a carving board. Let rest for 5 minutes, then cut into thick slices. Then remove the risotto from the heat and add the remaining butter. Mix well, then stir in the Parmesan until it melts. Put a scoop of risotto on each plate and add the chicken slices. Garnish with lemon wedges and thyme sprigs and serve at once.

IF YOU DON'T HAVE A GRILL PAN, YOU CAN COOK THE CHICKEN UNDER A BROILER INSTEAD, REDUCING THE HEAT FOR THE FINAL 15 MINUTES.

SHREDDED SPINACH AND HAM RISOTTO

SERVES 4

5 cups fresh young spinach leaves

4 oz/115 g cooked ham

4 cups chicken stock

1 tbsp olive oil

3 tbsp butter

1 small onion, finely chopped

generous 1³/₈ cups risotto rice

²/₃ cup dry white wine

¹/₄ cup light cream

³/₄ cup freshly grated Parmesan or Grana Padano cheese

salt and pepper

Wash the spinach well and slice into thin shreds. Cut the ham into thin strips.

Bring the stock to a boil in a pan, then reduce the heat and keep simmering gently over low heat while you are cooking the risotto.

Heat the oil with 2 tablespoons of the butter in a deep pan over medium heat until the butter has melted. Add the onion and cook, stirring occasionally, for 5 minutes, or until soft and starting to turn golden. Do not brown.

Reduce the heat, add the rice, and mix to coat in oil and butter. Cook, stirring constantly, for 2–3 minutes, or until the grains are translucent.

Add the wine and cook, stirring constantly, for 1 minute until reduced.

Gradually add the hot stock, a ladleful at a time. Stir constantly and add more liquid as the rice absorbs each addition. Increase the heat to medium so that the liquid bubbles. Cook for 20 minutes, or until all the liquid is absorbed and the rice is creamy. Add the spinach and ham with the last ladleful of stock.

Remove the risotto from the heat and add the remaining butter and the cream. Mix well, then stir in the Parmesan until it melts. Season to taste and serve at once.

FOR A SPICIER FLAVOR, YOU COULD SUBSTITUTE SALAMI FOR THE HAM. MAKE SURE THAT YOU PEEL OFF ANY RIND BEFORE CUTTING THE SLICES INTO STRIPS.

SAUSAGE AND BELL PEPPER RISOTTO

SERVES 4

8 sausages, sweet and/or spicy

1 red bell pepper, seeded and cut into 8 pieces

1 green bell pepper, seeded and cut into 8 pieces

1 onion, thickly sliced

4 tbsp olive oil

4 cups beef stock

3 tbsp butter

1 small onion, finely chopped

generous 1 3/8 cups risotto rice

2/3 cup red wine

3/4 cup freshly grated Parmesan or Grana Padano cheese

salt and pepper

fresh rosemary sprigs, to garnish

Preheat the oven to 375°F/190°C. Place the sausages in a large, shallow ovenproof dish. Scatter the bell peppers and sliced onion around the sausages and sprinkle with 3 tablespoons of the olive oil. Cook the sausages and vegetables in the oven for 20–30 minutes, turning occasionally.

Bring the stock to a boil in a pan, then reduce the heat and keep simmering gently over low heat while you are cooking the risotto.

Heat the remaining oil with 2 tablespoons of the butter in a deep pan over medium heat until the butter has melted. Add the chopped onion and cook, stirring occasionally, for 5 minutes, or until soft and starting to turn golden. Do not brown.

Reduce the heat, add the rice, and mix to coat in oil and butter. Cook, stirring constantly, for 2–3 minutes, or until the grains are translucent.

Add the wine and cook, stirring constantly, for 1 minute until reduced.

Gradually add the hot stock, a ladleful at a time. Stir constantly and add more liquid as the rice absorbs each addition. Increase the heat to medium so that the liquid bubbles. Cook for 20 minutes, or until all the liquid is absorbed and the rice is creamy. Season to taste.

Remove the risotto from the heat and add the remaining butter. Mix well, then stir in the Parmesan until it melts. Arrange a large scoop of risotto on each plate and sprinkle with bell peppers and onions. Place two sausages per person on either side of the risotto, garnish with rosemary sprigs, and serve at once.

FOR AN EVEN MORE COLORFUL PRESENTATION, USE A SLICED RED ONION WITH THE BELL PEPPERS. ITS LESS SHARP AND SLIGHTLY SWEETER FLAVOR WILL ALSO COMPLEMENT THE DISH.

CHICKEN, MUSHROOM, AND CASHEW RISOTTO

SERVES 4

generous 5¹/₂ cups chicken stock

2 oz/55 g butter

1 onion, chopped

9 oz/250 g skinless, boneless chicken breasts, diced

generous 1⁵/₈ cups risotto rice

1 tsp ground turmeric

²/₃ cup white wine

2³/₄ oz/75 g cremini mushrooms, sliced

scant ¹/₃ cup cashews, halved

salt and pepper

To garnish

wild arugula

fresh Parmesan cheese shavings

fresh basil leaves

Bring the stock to a boil in a pan, then reduce the heat and keep simmering gently over low heat while you are cooking the risotto.

Melt the butter in a large pan over medium heat. Add the onion and cook, stirring occasionally, for 5 minutes, or until softened. Add the chicken and cook, stirring frequently, for an additional 5 minutes.

Reduce the heat, add the rice, and mix to coat in butter. Cook, stirring constantly, for 2–3 minutes, or until the grains are translucent.

Stir in the turmeric, then add the wine. Cook, stirring constantly, for 1 minute until reduced.

Gradually add the hot stock, a ladleful at a time. Stir constantly and add more liquid as the rice absorbs each addition. Increase the heat to medium so that the liquid bubbles. Cook for 20 minutes, or until all the liquid is absorbed and the rice is creamy.

About 3 minutes before the end of the cooking time, stir in the mushrooms and cashews. Season to taste.

Arrange the arugula leaves on 4 individual serving plates. Remove the risotto from the heat and spoon it over the arugula. Sprinkle over the Parmesan shavings and basil leaves and serve.

THE CREMINI MUSHROOM IS A VARIETY OF THE COMMON CULTIVATED MUSHROOM AND IS WIDELY AVAILABLE. THE CAPS MAY BE BROWN OR CREAMY WHITE. THEY NEED ONLY TO BE WIPED AND SHOULD NOT BE PEELED.

This is the chapter for those who love to host elegant dinner parties and delight their guests with sophisticated and luxurious dishes. These are also the recipes to turn to if your love of fine food is matched by your love of cooking and you long to try something different and exciting. Here too, you will find mouthwatering dishes for special occasions and celebrations—after all, what could be more appropriate for a birthday dinner than Champagne, or for St Valentine's Day than lobster?

Certainly, some of these recipes include the most luxurious and extravagant ingredients for those times when only the very best will do. The French author Colette wrote that you pay for the weight of truffles in gold, which may be only the slightest of exaggerations, but they are undeniably gorgeous.

However, not all of these risotti require an unlimited budget. As always with Italian cooking,

PART FIVE
A GOURMET SELECTION

it is the quality rather than the price of the ingredients that really matters. Imaginative combinations of flavors and using peak condition produce will always create magical and unforgettable meals.

Then there is that extra special ingredient required for every kind of risotto—the tender loving attention of the cook. You cannot just rely on spending a fortune at the delicatessen to achieve results. In fact, it may be even more important to hover, spoon in hand, with a beady eye fixed on the pan when preparing these marvelous dishes—some of which are traditional Italian specialties while others are modern innovative recipes.

CHAMPAGNE RISOTTO

SERVES 4–6

3 cups light chicken stock

2 tbsp vegetable oil

4 oz/115 g butter

2 shallots, finely chopped

scant 1 1/2 cups
risotto rice

about 2 1/2 cups
Champagne or dry
sparkling white wine

generous 1/2 cup freshly
grated Parmesan cheese

salt and pepper

4–6 large cooked shrimp,
to garnish (optional)

Bring the stock to a boil in a pan, then reduce the heat and keep simmering gently over low heat while you are cooking the risotto.

Heat the oil and half the butter in a large heavy-bottom pan over medium heat. Add the shallots and cook, stirring occasionally, for 2 minutes, or until softened.

Reduce the heat, add the rice, and mix to coat in oil and butter. Cook, stirring constantly, for 2–3 minutes, or until the grains are translucent.

Pour in half the Champagne; it will bubble and steam rapidly. Cook, stirring constantly, for 1–2 minutes until reduced.

Gradually add the hot stock, a ladleful at a time. Stir constantly and add more liquid as the rice absorbs each addition. Increase the heat to medium so that the liquid bubbles. Cook for 20 minutes, or until all the liquid is absorbed.

Stir in the remaining Champagne and cook for an additional 2–3 minutes until the liquid is absorbed and the rice is creamy.

Remove the risotto from the heat and add the remaining butter. Mix well, then stir in the Parmesan until it melts. Season to taste with salt and pepper.

Spoon the risotto into serving bowls and garnish each portion with a shrimp, if you like. Serve at once.

TAKE CARE WHEN ADDING SPARKLING WINE TO A HOT PAN, AS IT WILL FROTH UP FAR MORE VIGOROUSLY THAN STILL WINE. DEPENDING ON THE SIZE OF THE PAN, IT MAY BE BETTER TO ADD IT IN TWO STAGES.

TRUFFLE RISOTTO

SERVES 6

5 cups chicken or
vegetable stock

2 leeks

4 oz/115 g butter

scant 1 1/2 cups
risotto rice

1/4 cup dry white
vermouth or white wine

1/2 cup heavy cream

freshly grated nutmeg

1 cup freshly grated
Parmesan cheese

4–6 oz/115–175 g fresh
black truffles,
brushed clean

1/4–1/3 cup truffle oil
(optional)

salt and 1/4–1/2 tsp ground
white pepper

Bring the stock to a boil in a pan, then reduce the heat and keep simmering gently over low heat while you are cooking the risotto.

Slice the leeks in half lengthwise, then shred thinly. Heat half the butter in a heavy-bottom pan over medium heat. Add the leeks and cook for 1 minute, or until just starting to soften.

Reduce the heat, add the rice, and mix to coat in butter. Cook, stirring constantly, for 2–3 minutes, or until the grains are translucent.

Add the vermouth and cook, stirring constantly, for 1 minute until reduced.

Gradually add the hot stock, a ladleful at a time. Stir constantly and add more liquid as the rice absorbs each addition. Increase the heat to medium so that the liquid bubbles. Cook for 20 minutes, or until all the liquid is absorbed and the rice is creamy.

Just before the end of the cooking time, stir in the cream. Season with a little nutmeg, salt, and white pepper. Continue cooking for 3–4 minutes until the liquid is absorbed.

Remove the risotto from the heat and add the remaining butter. Mix well, then stir in the Parmesan until it melts. Spoon into serving dishes and shave equal amounts of truffle over each portion. Drizzle over a little truffle oil, if using, and serve at once.

WHITE TRUFFLES CAN ALSO BE USED TO MAKE THIS DISH. BOUGHT FRESH, BOTH BLACK AND WHITE TRUFFLES HAVE AN INCOMPARABLE FLAVOR, BUT ARE EXPENSIVE AND THEIR SEASON IS SHORT. AN ALTERNATIVE IS TO USE THE PRESERVED VARIETY.

LEMON AND VEAL RISOTTO

SERVES 4

4 cups chicken stock

3 tbsp olive oil

3 tbsp butter

1 small onion, finely chopped

generous 1 3/8 cups risotto rice

scant 1 cup dry white wine

1 lb/450 g veal scallops, beaten thin

1 tsp dried oregano

1 tsp dried thyme

2 tbsp lemon juice

3 tbsp water

3/4 cup freshly grated Parmesan or Grana Padano cheese

salt and pepper

thinly pared rind of 2 lemons, to garnish

Bring the stock to a boil in a pan, then reduce the heat and keep simmering gently over low heat while you are cooking the risotto.

Heat 1 tablespoon of the oil with 2 tablespoons of the butter in a pan over medium heat until the butter has melted. Add the onion and cook, stirring occasionally, for 5 minutes, or until soft and turning golden. Do not brown.

Reduce the heat, add the rice, and mix to coat in oil and butter. Cook, stirring constantly, for 2–3 minutes, or until the grains are translucent.

Add ⅔ cup of the wine and cook, stirring constantly, for 1 minute until reduced.

Gradually add the hot stock, a ladleful at a time. Stir constantly and add more liquid as the rice absorbs each addition. Increase the heat to medium so that the liquid bubbles. Cook for 20 minutes, or until all the liquid is absorbed and the rice is creamy. Season to taste.

Meanwhile, sprinkle the remaining oil over the veal. Rub in the herbs and salt and pepper. Heat a nonstick skillet over high heat and brown the veal quickly, turning once. Pour over the lemon juice, remaining wine, and the water. Bring to a boil, then reduce the heat. Cover and let simmer gently for 15 minutes.

When the meat is cooked through, transfer to a serving dish and garnish with lemon rind.

Remove the risotto from the heat and add the remaining butter. Mix well, then stir in the Parmesan until it melts. Adjust the seasoning, if necessary, and serve at once with the veal.

To prepare the veal, wrap in plastic wrap and beat gently with the flat side of a meat mallet or the side of a rolling pin. Try to keep the thickness even.

BEET, DRIED CHERRY, AND RED WINE RISOTTO

SERVES 4–6

5 cups chicken or
vegetable stock

generous 1³/₈ cups
dried sour cherries or
dried cranberries

1 cup fruity red wine, such
as Valpolicella

3 tbsp olive oil

1 large red onion,
finely chopped

2 celery stalks,
finely chopped

¹/₂ tsp dried thyme

1 garlic clove,
finely chopped

generous 1⁵/₈ cups
risotto rice

4 cooked fresh
beet, diced

2 tbsp chopped fresh dill

2 tbsp snipped
fresh chives

salt and pepper

generous ¹/₂ cup freshly
grated Parmesan cheese,
to serve (optional)

Bring the stock to a boil in a pan, then reduce the heat and keep simmering gently over low heat while you are cooking the risotto.

Place the sour cherries in a pan with the wine and bring to a boil, then reduce the heat and let simmer for 2–3 minutes until slightly reduced. Remove from the heat and set aside.

Heat the olive oil in a large, heavy-bottom pan over medium heat. Add the onion, celery, and thyme and cook, stirring occasionally, for 3 minutes, or until just starting to soften. Add the garlic and cook for 30 seconds.

Reduce the heat, add the rice, and mix to coat in oil. Cook, stirring constantly, for 2–3 minutes, or until the grains are translucent.

Gradually add the hot stock, a ladleful at a time. Stir constantly and add more liquid as the rice absorbs each addition. Increase the heat to medium so that the liquid bubbles. Cook for 20 minutes, or until the liquid is absorbed and the rice is creamy.

Halfway through the risotto cooking time, remove the cherries from the wine with a slotted spoon and add to the risotto with the beet and half the wine. Continue adding the stock and the remaining wine.

Stir in the dill and chives and season, if necessary. Serve with the Parmesan, if you like.

As well as being colorful, beet has a deliciously sweet flavor that is perfectly balanced by the sharpness of sour cherries or cranberries. Make sure you don't buy pickled beet.

FENNEL RISOTTO WITH VODKA

SERVES 4–6

generous 5½ cups
chicken or vegetable stock

2 large fennel bulbs

2 tbsp vegetable oil

3 oz/85 g butter

I large onion,
finely chopped

generous 1⅝ cups
risotto rice

⅔ cup vodka

5–6 tbsp lemon juice

generous ½ cup freshly
grated Parmesan cheese

salt and pepper

Bring the stock to a boil in a pan, then reduce the heat and keep simmering over low heat while you are cooking the risotto.

Trim the fennel, reserving the fronds for the garnish, if desired. Cut the bulbs in half lengthwise and remove the V-shaped cores. Coarsely chop the flesh. (If you like, add any of the fennel trimmings to the stock for extra flavor.)

Heat the oil with half the butter in a large heavy-bottom pan over medium heat until the butter has melted. Add the onion and fennel and cook, stirring occasionally, for 5 minutes, or until the vegetables are softened.

Reduce the heat, add the rice, and mix to coat in oil and butter. Cook, stirring constantly, for 2–3 minutes, or until the grains are translucent.

Pour in the vodka and cook, stirring constantly, for I minute until reduced.

Gradually add the hot stock, a ladleful at a time. Stir constantly and add more liquid as the rice absorbs each addition. Increase the heat to medium so that the liquid bubbles. Cook for 20 minutes, or until all the liquid is absorbed and the rice is creamy. Season to taste.

Remove the risotto from the heat and add the remaining butter and lemon juice to taste. Mix well, then stir in the Parmesan until it melts. Serve at once, garnished with the reserved fennel fronds, if using.

YOU CAN SUBSTITUTE LEMON-FLAVORED VODKA FOR THE PLAIN, IF YOU CAN FIND IT, BUT, IF SO, YOU MAY NEED TO ADJUST THE AMOUNT OF LEMON JUICE THAT YOU ADD AT THE END OF COOKING.

LOBSTER RISOTTO

SERVES 2

1 cooked lobster, about
14 oz–1 lb/400–450 g

2¹/₂ cups fish stock

1 tbsp olive oil

2 oz/55 g butter

¹/₂ onion, finely chopped

1 garlic clove,
finely chopped

1 tsp chopped fresh
thyme leaves

generous ³/₄ cup
risotto rice

²/₃ cup sparkling
white wine

1 tsp green or pink
peppercorns in
brine, drained and
coarsely chopped

1 tbsp chopped
fresh parsley

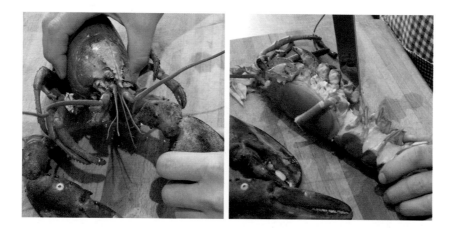

FOR A SLIGHTLY LESS
EXTRAVAGANT VERSION,
YOU COULD SUBSTITUTE
1 LB/450 G JUMBO
SHRIMP FOR THE
LOBSTER. IF YOU PEEL
THEM YOURSELF, YOU
CAN USE THE HEADS
AND SHELLS TO MAKE A
DELICATELY FLAVORED
SHELLFISH STOCK.

To prepare the lobster, remove the claws by twisting them. Crack the claws using the back of a large knife and set aside. Split the body lengthwise. Remove and discard the intestinal vein, the stomach sac, and the spongy gills. Remove the meat from the tail and coarsely chop. Set aside with the claws.

Bring the stock to a boil in a pan, then reduce the heat and keep simmering gently over low heat while you are cooking the risotto.

Heat the oil with half the butter in a large pan over medium heat. Add the onion and cook, stirring occasionally, for 5 minutes until softened. Add the garlic and cook for an additional 30 seconds. Stir in the thyme.

Reduce the heat, add the rice, and mix to coat in butter and oil. Cook, stirring constantly, for 2–3 minutes, or until the grains are translucent.

Stir in the wine and cook, stirring constantly, for 1 minute until reduced. Gradually add the hot stock, a ladleful at a time. Stir constantly and add more liquid as the rice absorbs each addition. Increase the heat to medium so that the liquid bubbles. Cook for 20 minutes, or until all the liquid is absorbed and the rice is creamy.

Five minutes before the end of cooking time, add the lobster meat and claws.

Remove the pan from the heat and stir in the peppercorns, remaining butter, and the parsley. Spoon onto warmed plates and serve at once.

INDEX